Dear Friends,

Over the past 16 years, I have had the wonderful pleasure of helping thousands of people reach their personal goals for weight loss and well-being. During that time, our Program has continually evolved to reflect the latest research on strategies for weight loss success. What hasn't changed is our clients' need for convenience and desire for great-tasting food.

As a Jenny Craig Client, I know you depend on simple solutions to manage your meals. Busy, working, crunched for time—isn't that how you'd describe your day? That's why we designed this cookbook: To give you a plan for getting the most hectic meal—dinner—on the table in minutes. Whether you're cooking for one or a family of four, you'll have a month's worth of menus to satisfy the hungriest of appetites in a healthy way! And regardless of where you are in your program, you'll have dozens of ideas for adding variety to your Menus.

Let this cookbook be your guide for planning healthy, lowfat meals. Let it also be a model for the pleasure of eating. As you learn quick tricks for trimming the fat from your favorite recipes, be equally aware of easy ways to expand their flavors. You'll be amazed at how deliciously simple it can be!

Bon appetit!

Jenny Craig

Table Of Contents

A Cookbook Designed For You

Does your lifestyle leave you little time for menu planning, grocery shopping and food preparation? Do you find it a challenge to cut down on fat and capitalize on flavor in your everyday cooking? Then this cookbook is for you!

Designed by staff Registered Dietitians, Jenny Craig's *30 Meals in 30 Minutes* offers 30 pre-planned, nutritionally balanced menus, each featuring:

- A dinner entrée/side dish or salad/dessert
- A recipe cook time of 30 minutes or less
- A nutritional analysis for each recipe
- A list of exchanges for each recipe
- A "Quick Meal Countdown" to coordinate every dish
- "At The Market" and "Kitchen Staples" lists for convenient shopping

How To Use This Cookbook

Weight loss or weight maintenance, you can tailor the menus and recipes in this cookbook to match your personal goals. For instance, if you are:

Following A Jenny Craig Weight Loss Menu

Scan each 30-minute menu and refer to our "Recipe Index" for salads, side dishes and desserts. Cooking for family or friends? Pick a 30-minute menu and adjust it to your Dining Out Dinner exchanges.

Reaching Your Halfway Weight Goal

Slip some new recipes into your Pyramid Menu. Either use one of our 30-minute menus in its entirety, or choose an entrée, side dish or dessert that fits into your family's favorite meal.

Maintaining Your Weight

Add a little punch to your Maintenance Menu. Use a 30-minute menu as your base, and then increase the portion sizes to match your calorie level.

Make Dinners A Cinch

Dinner doesn't have to be a last-minute scramble. All it takes is a little advance planning using these three time-saving techniques:

Once A Month

Make a grocery run to stock your pantry with staple items: core foods such as beans, rice, pasta, canned fruits and vegetables; flavor enhancers like herbs/spices, oils/vinegars, sauces/condiments; emergency meal makers such as canned tuna/chicken, cream of mushroom soup, boxed rice/noodle mixes and marinara sauce.

And don't forget the freezer—it's a great place to store staples for dinner in a pinch. Besides old standbys like peas and carrots, include items that give an entrée international flair, such as Italian/Mexican/Oriental vegetable medleys. Read the labels on sauced combos, which can add extra calories and fat. Land or sea, lowfat frozen options are available. Look for fish filets, shrimp, scallops and chicken breast patties—all minus the batter/heavy breading.

Follow our "Pantry List" and you'll have nearly everything you need for our 30-minute menus.

Once A Week

Shop for fresh foods: seasonal fruits and vegetables, bakery breads and rolls, lean meats, poultry, fish and seafood, and reduced fat dairy products.

Use our "At The Market List" to create your own weekly shopping list, and to quickly check off the ingredients you need for each 30-minute menu.

Once A Day

Refer to our "Quick Meal Countdown" list for a step-by-step plan for getting a complete dinner on the table.

Kitchen Shortcuts

When Speed Is Of The Essence

1. Pick quick-cook meat and fish cuts: boneless, skinless chicken breasts; turkey cutlets; pork chops; fish filets.

2. Stock ready-to-use staples: seasoned, chopped tomatoes; jarred tomatoes/meat sauces; chili/barbecued beans; frozen vegetable medleys.

3. Choose convenient cheeses: shredded, reduced fat cheddar/mozzarella/Parmesan; sliced, reduced fat Swiss; crumbled, reduced fat feta.

4. Select prewashed and cut produce: salad bags, cabbage/broccoli slaw, vegetables for stir-fry and seasonal fruits.

5. Rely on ready-to-use desserts: reduced fat pound cake; shortcake; fat-free pudding; light ice cream; sorbet.

Build A Stable Of Staples

Look to this list of core foods and flavor enhancers to help you create an entire meal from start to finish, or supplement a quick trip to the market. Keep a copy of this list close by as a convenient way to note what needs to be replenished during your next monthly grocery trip.

Pantry List

Grains And Beans
- ❑ Beans (black/cannellini/chili/kidney/lima)
- ❑ Corn bread mix
- ❑ Couscous
- ❑ Flavored, boxed rice mixes
- ❑ Orzo
- ❑ Pasta (fettuccini/linguini/macaroni/penne)
- ❑ Rice (arborio/brown/white)

Canned
- ❑ Chicken/vegetable broth
- ❑ Fruits (applesauce/peaches/pears)
- ❑ Soups (celery/chicken/cream of mushroom/tomato)
- ❑ Tomatoes (Italian/Mexican-style/stewed)
- ❑ Tomato/marinara sauce
- ❑ Tuna/salmon/clams

Frozen
- ❑ Blueberries
- ❑ Chopped broccoli/spinach, peas, green beans
- ❑ Fat-free, nondairy whipped topping
- ❑ Light ice cream/frozen yogurt
- ❑ Light pound cake
- ❑ Melon medley
- ❑ Mixed vegetable medleys
- ❑ Sorbet
- ❑ Strawberries
- ❑ Vegetable medleys

Herbs/Spices
- ❑ Basil
- ❑ Chili powder
- ❑ Cilantro
- ❑ Cinnamon
- ❑ Dill weed
- ❑ Garlic powder
- ❑ Ginger
- ❑ Herb blends
- ❑ Oregano
- ❑ Parsley
- ❑ Rosemary
- ❑ Thyme

Oils
- ❑ Canola oil
- ❑ Corn oil
- ❑ Nonstick vegetable spray
- ❑ Olive oil
- ❑ Reduced fat salad dressings
- ❑ Safflower oil
- ❑ Sesame oil
- ❑ Soybean oil

Condiments
- ❑ Catsup
- ❑ Dijon mustard
- ❑ Fat-free salad dressings (blue cheese/Caesar/ranch/vinaigrette)
- ❑ Honey mustard
- ❑ Light mayonnaise

Nuts
- ❑ Almonds
- ❑ Peanuts
- ❑ Pine nuts
- ❑ Walnuts

Vinegars
- ❑ Balsamic
- ❑ Cider
- ❑ Raspberry
- ❑ Red wine

Sweeteners
- ❑ Brown sugar
- ❑ Honey
- ❑ Light fruit spreads

Miscellaneous
- ❑ Cornstarch
- ❑ Olives
- ❑ Salsa
- ❑ Soy sauce

Other
- ❑ _____
- ❑ _____
- ❑ _____
- ❑ _____

Streamline Your Shopping

What's the number-one tip for ensuring that you'll bring home a healthy bag of groceries? Take a list. Here's one to guide you through the weekly market maze. As you navigate the aisles, focus on seasonal fruits and vegetables, whole grains, lean meats/fish and reduced fat dairy products, which are the mainstays of a balanced menu.

At The Market List

Bakery
- ❏ Breadsticks
- ❏ Corn tortillas
- ❏ Flour tortillas
- ❏ Italian bread
- ❏ Pita bread
- ❏ Prebaked pizza crust
- ❏ Whole-wheat rolls

Meats And Poultry Sections
- ❏ Beef loin (kebobs/steaks)
- ❏ Beef round (medallions/strips)
- ❏ Beef sirloin
   (cubes/kebobs/steaks)
- ❏ Chicken breast (boneless/ground/
   skinless/tenders)
- ❏ Pork loin (bone-in/boneless
   chops)
- ❏ Pork tenderloin (sliced/whole)
- ❏ Turkey breast
   (ground/scallops/strips/whole)

Fish And Seafood Section
- ❏ Crab
- ❏ Halibut
- ❏ Roughy
- ❏ Salmon
- ❏ Scallops
- ❏ Shrimp

Dairy Case
- ❏ Eggs/egg substitute
- ❏ Flavored, nonfat yogurt
- ❏ Lowfat cottage cheese
- ❏ Nonfat milk
- ❏ Orange juice
- ❏ Parmesan cheese
- ❏ Reduced fat cheddar cheese
- ❏ Reduced fat cream cheese
- ❏ Reduced fat feta cheese
- ❏ Reduced fat jack cheese
- ❏ Reduced fat sour cream
- ❏ Reduced fat Swiss cheese

Produce
- ❏ Apples
- ❏ Asparagus
- ❏ Bananas
- ❏ Blueberries
- ❏ Broccoli
- ❏ Carrots (baby/sliced/whole)
- ❏ Cranberries (dried)
- ❏ Garlic
- ❏ Grapefruit
- ❏ Green beans
- ❏ Kiwi
- ❏ Lemons
- ❏ Limes
- ❏ Melon
- ❏ Nectarines
- ❏ Onions
- ❏ Oranges
- ❏ Peaches
- ❏ Pears
- ❏ Peppers
- ❏ Pineapple
- ❏ Potatoes (red/russet)
- ❏ Prewashed vegetables
- ❏ Raspberries
- ❏ Salad greens
- ❏ Spinach
- ❏ Squash (summer/winter)
- ❏ Tomatoes
   (garden/roma/teardrop)
- ❏ Zucchini

Fresh Herbs
- ❏ Basil
- ❏ Cilantro
- ❏ Dill
- ❏ Oregano
- ❏ Parsley
- ❏ Rosemary
- ❏ Thyme

Other
- ❏ _____
- ❏ _____
- ❏ _____
- ❏ _____
- ❏ _____

Broiled Orange Roughy with Mango Salsa

Fish and Shellfish

Seafood Risotto
Broccoli with Lemon
Whole-Wheat Dinner Rolls
Cappuccino Mousse

Quick Meal Countdown:
1. Make Cappuccino Mousse and refrigerate.
2. Prepare Seafood Risotto.
3. Microwave broccoli.
4. Just before serving, garnish risotto with cheese and broccoli with lemon wedges.

Seafood Risotto
Prep Time: 5 minutes
Cook Time: 30 minutes

Ingredients:
1	Tbl olive oil
1/2	cup finely chopped onion
1	clove garlic
1	cup long grain rice (arborio)
2	cups chicken broth, divided
1/2	cup diced zucchini
1/2	lb raw medium shrimp, peeled, deveined and halved lengthwise
1/2	lb scallops (quartered if large)
1/2	cup frozen peas, thawed
1/4	cup minced parsley
3	Tbls grated Parmesan cheese, plus additional for serving

Directions:
Heat oil in large, heavy skillet. Sauté onion and garlic over medium heat until soft. Add rice and sauté until opaque, about 3 minutes. Add 1 cup broth and bring to a boil. Cover and simmer about 8 minutes or until liquid is absorbed. Add remaining broth and zucchini; cover and simmer 3 minutes. Add shrimp, scallops and peas. Simmer, covered, about 10 minutes, stirring once. Stir in parsley and cook about 5 minutes or until the liquid is absorbed, rice is tender and seafood is opaque throughout (watch carefully at this point as rice may stick). Sprinkle with Parmesan cheese. Yield: 4 servings.

Per Serving:	420 calories, 53 g carbohydrate, 29 g protein, 8 g fat, 107 mg cholesterol, 918 mg sodium
Exchanges:	3 very lean meats, 3 starches, 1 vegetable, 2 fats

Cappuccino Mousse

Prep Time: 10 minutes
Cook Time: 2 minutes
Chill Time: 15 minutes

Ingredients:
1   envelope Knox® Unflavored Gelatine
1/4 cup strong coffee, cooled
1   cup fat-free cappuccino yogurt
1/4 cup sugar
1 1/4 cups prepared fat-free, nondairy
      whipped topping, divided
4   cinnamon sticks, for garnish

Directions:
Sprinkle gelatine over coffee in saucepan; let stand 1 minute. Stir over low heat until gelatine completely dissolves, about 2 minutes. Blend yogurt and sugar in blender at high speed until smooth. Add gelatine mixture; process until blended. Fold 1 cup whipped topping into yogurt mixture. Spoon into individual dessert dishes. Refrigerate for 15 minutes before serving. Garnish with remaining whipped topping and cinnamon sticks. Yield: 4 servings.

At The Market

1	onion
1	bulb garlic
1	zucchini
1/2	lb raw medium, cleaned shrimp
1/2	lb raw scallops
1	bunch parsley
1	bunch broccoli
1	lemon
1	bag whole-wheat dinner rolls
1	(8-oz) carton fat-free cappuccino yogurt

Per Serving: 148 calories, 22 g carbohydrate, 5 g protein, 5 g fat, 1 mg cholesterol, 49 mg sodium

Exchanges: 1 1/2 starches, 1 fat

Kitchen Staples:
• olive oil • arborio rice • chicken broth • frozen peas • Parmesan cheese •
• unflavored gelatin • instant coffee • sugar • fat-free, nondairy whipped topping •
• cinnamon sticks •

Halibut in Red Pepper Sauce

Couscous
Zucchini with Italian Herbs
Cinnamon Peaches

Quick Meal Countdown:

1. Prepare Cinnamon Peaches and chill.
2. Broil halibut.
3. Cook couscous as directed on package.
4. Prepare Red Pepper Sauce.
5. Microwave zucchini, top with herbs.

Halibut in Red Pepper Sauce
Prep Time: 5 minutes
Cook Time: 20 minutes

Ingredients:
Steaks:

1	lb halibut steaks
1/8	tsp salt
1/8	tsp pepper
1	Tbl margarine, melted

Sauce:

1 1/2	Tbls margarine
1	cup minced onion
2	red bell peppers, cut into thin strips
1	lb can of tomatoes, undrained, cut up
1/2	tsp salt
1/8	tsp red pepper

Directions:
Preheat broiler. Sprinkle steaks with salt and pepper; brush with margarine. Broil an additional 5 to 8 minutes or until fish is firm, turns translucent to opaque. In a saucepan, melt margarine, add onions and peppers and cook just until tender, about 5 minutes. Mix in remaining ingredients, simmer, stirring occasionally for 10 minutes. Place halibut on a serving platter and spoon sauce over. Yield: 4 servings.

Per Serving:	243 calories, 11 g carbohydrate, 26 g protein, 10 g fat, 36 mg cholesterol, 688 mg sodium
Exchanges:	3 very lean meats, 2 vegetables, 2 fats

Cinnamon Peaches

Prep Time: 5 minutes
Cook Time: 10 minutes

Ingredients:
2	Tbls light corn syrup
1/4	tsp McCormick® Ground Cinnamon
1/4	tsp fresh lemon juice
2	(16 oz each) cans sliced peaches, drained; or 6 fresh peaches, sliced

Directions:
In medium saucepan, combine corn syrup, cinnamon and lemon juice. Add peaches and simmer, uncovered, 10 minutes (If using fresh peaches, peel before slicing). Spoon into serving dishes and serve hot or cold. Yield: 4 servings.

Per Serving: 92 calories, 24 g carbohydrate, 1 g protein, 0 g fat, 0 mg cholesterol, 12 mg sodium
Exchanges: 1 1/2 fruits

At The Market

1	lb halibut steaks
1	onion
2	red bell peppers
1	lb zucchini
1	lemon
2	(16 oz each) cans of peaches or 6 fresh peaches

Kitchen Staples:
• salt • pepper • margarine • canned tomatoes • red pepper • couscous •
• Italian herb blend • light corn syrup • ground cinnamon •

Shrimp and Vegetable Stir-Fry

Spicy-Tangy Beef Soup
Steamed White Rice
Almond Cookies

Quick Meal Countdown:

1. Prepare soup and let simmer.
2. Steam rice.
3. Prepare Shrimp and Vegetable Stir-Fry.
4. Serve Stir-Fry over rice.

Shrimp and Vegetable Stir-Fry
Prep Time: 5 minutes
Cook Time: 10 minutes

Ingredients:

1	lb raw, cleaned shrimp
1	tsp sesame oil
	Nonstick vegetable spray
1	(14-oz) package fresh stir-fry vegetables
1	cup fresh bean sprouts
1	tsp cornstarch, dissolved in 1/2 cup low-sodium chicken broth
2	tsps low-sodium soy sauce
1	tsp fresh lemon juice
1/4	tsp ground ginger
1/8	tsp garlic powder
2	green onions, diagonally sliced

Directions:

Rinse shrimp in cold water and pat dry with paper towels; set aside. Heat sesame oil in a wok or a large frying pan that has been coated with nonstick vegetable spray over high heat. When oil is hot, add the vegetables and bean sprouts. Cook uncovered, stirring continuously, for 3 to 4 minutes until colors of vegetables brighten. Push vegetables aside in wok or pan and add shrimp. Add cornstarch mixture along with soy sauce, lemon juice, ginger and garlic. Stir-fry 2 to 3 minutes until shrimp turns pink and becomes opaque. Serve at once, garnished with green onion slices. Yield: 4 servings.

Per Serving:	183 calories, 10 g carbohydrate, 27 g protein, 3 g fat, 173 mg cholesterol, 293 mg sodium
Exchanges:	3 very lean meats, 2 vegetables, 1/2 fat

Spicy-Tangy Beef Soup

Prep Time: 10 minutes
Cook Time: 20 minutes

Ingredients:

3/4	lb beef round tip steaks, 1/8-in to 1/4-in thick
1	(13 3/4 to 14 1/4 oz) can vegetable broth
1 1/2	cups water
1 3/4	cups sliced mushrooms
1	cup julienne carrots
3	Tbls low sodium soy sauce, divided
2	Tbls red wine vinegar
3/4	tsp crushed red pepper
1	oz uncooked angel hair pasta, broken up (approximately 1/4 cup)
2	Tbls cornstarch, dissolved in 1/4 cup water
1/4	cup sliced green onion

Directions:

Stack beef steaks, cut lengthwise into 1/4-inch strips. In 3-quart saucepan, combine broth, 1 1/2 cups water, mushrooms, carrots, 2 tablespoons low-sodium soy sauce, vinegar and red pepper. Bring to a boil; reduce heat and simmer uncovered for 5 minutes.

At The Market

1	*lb cleaned shrimp*
1	*(14-oz) package stir-fry vegetables*
1	*cup fresh bean sprouts*
1	*lemon*
1	*bunch green onions*
3/4	*lb beef round tip steaks*
1	*(8-oz) package fresh mushrooms*
1	*bunch fresh carrots*
1	*box almond cookies*

Add pasta; continue simmering 5 additional minutes. Stir in cornstarch mixture. Bring to a boil; cook and stir 1 minute. Stir beef into soup. Immediately remove from heat. Cover and let stand 5 minutes. Stir in remaining 1 tablespoon low-sodium soy sauce and green onions. Serve immediately. Yield: 4 servings.

Per Serving: 195 calories, 15 g carbohydrate, 22 g protein, 5 g fat, 52 mg cholesterol, 852 mg sodium

Exchanges: 2 lean meats, 1/2 starch, 1 vegetable

Kitchen Staples:

• sesame oil • nonstick vegetable spray • cornstarch • low-sodium chicken broth •
• low-sodium soy sauce • ground ginger • garlic powder • vegetable broth •
• red wine vinegar • crushed red pepper • angel hair pasta • instant white rice •

Broiled Orange Roughy with Mango Salsa

**Lemon Dijon Green Beans
Almondine
Parsley-New Potatoes
Raspberry Sorbet**

Quick Meal Countdown:

1. Prepare Mango Salsa and chill.
2. Preheat broiler and boil potatoes.
3. Broil orange roughy.
4. Prepare green beans.
5. Top fish with salsa, green beans with almonds and potatoes with parsley.

Broiled Orange Roughy with Mango Salsa
Prep Time: 10 minutes
Cook Time: 5 minutes

Ingredients:

1	ripe mango
1/8	tsp ground allspice
2	Tbls chopped green onion
4	tsps fresh lime juice
2	Tbls diced red bell pepper
4	(4-oz) orange roughy filets
	Nonstick vegetable spray
	Paprika

Directions:

Peel mango and dice into a small bowl. Mix together with allspice, green onion, lime juice and diced red bell pepper. Cover and chill. Preheat broiler. Rinse fish and pat dry with paper towels. Place on a shallow pan that has been coated with nonstick vegetable spray. Sprinkle lightly with paprika. Broil 3 to 4 inches from heat for approximately 5 minutes. Fish is done when it flakes easily with a fork. To serve, spoon 1/4 of the Mango Salsa over each filet.
Yield: 4 servings.

Per Serving: 118 calories, 10 g carbohydrate, 17 g protein, 1 g fat, 23 g cholesterol, 84 mg sodium
Exchanges: 3 very lean meats

Lemon Dijon Green Beans Almondine

Prep Time: 5 minutes
Cook Time: 5 minutes

Ingredients:

1/2	lb fresh or frozen whole green beans
1	Tbl margarine or butter
1	Tbl lemon juice
1	Tbl Grey Poupon® Dijon Mustard
1/4	tsp dried dill
1	Tbl Planters® Sliced Almonds, toasted

Directions:
Cook and stir beans in margarine or butter in a large skillet over medium-high heat to desired tenderness. Add lemon juice, mustard and dill; toss well and heat through. Sprinkle with almonds before serving. Yield: 4 servings.

At The Market

1	mango
1	bunch of green onions
1	lime
1	red bell pepper
4	(4-oz) orange roughy filets
1/2	lb fresh or frozen whole green beans
1	lemon
1	lb new potatoes
1	bunch parsley

Per Serving: 57 calories, 4 g carbohydrate, 2 g protein, 4 g fat, 0 mg cholesterol, 37 mg sodium
Exchanges: 1 vegetable, 1 fat

Kitchen Staples:

• allspice • nonstick vegetable spray • paprika • margarine or butter •
• Dijon mustard • dried dill • sliced almonds • raspberry sorbet •

Poached Salmon and Pasta

Mediterranean Asparagus
Lemon Bars

Quick Meal Countdown:
1. Prepare lemon bars as directed on box.
2. Prepare sauce for salmon and chill.
3. Cook salmon and simmer.
4. Cook pasta.
5. Boil asparagus.
6. Top salmon with sauce, and asparagus with olives, tomatoes and cheese.

Poached Salmon and Pasta
Prep Time: 10 minutes
Chill Time: 20 minutes
Cook Time: 25 minutes

Ingredients:
Cucumber-Mustard Sauce:
- 1/2 cup cucumber, peeled, seeded and minced
- 1/4 cup plain nonfat yogurt
- 1 Tbl Dijon mustard
- 1 Tbl capers
- 1 1/2 tsps dried dill weed
- Pinch of white pepper

Salmon:
- 2 cloves garlic, finely minced or pressed
- 1 medium onion, chopped
- Nonstick vegetable spray
- 3/4 cup carrots, chopped
- 1/2 cup celery, thinly sliced
- 1 cup low-sodium vegetable broth
- 1/4 cup white wine
- 2 Tbls fresh lemon juice
- 4 (4-oz) salmon filets
- 1 cup tomatoes, peeled and chopped

Pasta:
- 1 (8-oz) package angel hair pasta
- 1 lemon, cut into wedges for garnish

Directions:
For the sauce, drain the cucumber to remove any excess water. Add remaining ingredients. Combine thoroughly and chill for at least 1 hour. Stir before serving. Makes 4 servings of 3 tablespoons each.

For the salmon, sauté the garlic and onions until translucent in a nonstick skillet or in a skillet coated with nonstick vegetable spray. Add the carrots and celery, stir, and cook for

1 to 2 minutes. Add the vegetable broth, stir, and simmer for 7 minutes more. Add the wine and lemon juice to the skillet; stir to mix. Place the salmon on top of the vegetables, add the tomatoes, and cover. Simmer for 15 minutes until salmon is tender.

Cook the pasta according to the package directions. Drain. Serve the salmon with vegetables over the pasta, top with the Cucumber-Mustard Sauce, and garnish with lemon wedges. Yield: 4 servings.

Per Serving:	278 calories, 25 g carbohydrate, 29 g protein, 6 g fat, 79 mg cholesterol, 254 mg sodium
Exchanges:	3 lean meats, 1 starch, 1 vegetable

Mediterranean Asparagus

Prep Time: 5 minutes
Cook Time: 3 minutes

Ingredients:

1 1/2	cups water
1	lb asparagus, ends trimmed
4	Tbls sliced olives
1	Tbl sun-dried tomatoes in oil
2	Tbls grated Parmesan cheese

At The Market

1	cucumber
1	(8-oz) carton plain nonfat yogurt
2	bulbs garlic
1	onion
1	bunch carrots
1	bunch celery
2	lemons
4	(4-oz) salmon filets
1	lb tomatoes
1	lb asparagus
1	(16 1/2-oz) box lemon bar mix

Directions.

Bring water to a boil in a large saucepan. Add asparagus, cook 3 minutes to desired tenderness. Drain. Top with olives, tomatoes and cheese. Serve immediately.
Yield: 4 servings.

Per Serving:	57 calories, 3 g carbohydrate, 4 g protein, 3 g fat, 2 mg cholesterol, 189 mg sodium
Exchanges:	1 vegetable, 1 fat

Kitchen Staples:

• Dijon mustard • capers • dried dill weed • white pepper •
nonstick vegetable spray • low-sodium vegetable broth • white wine •
angel hair pasta • olives • sun-dried tomatoes in oil • Parmesan cheese •

Scaloppine of Sole with Herbs

Angel Hair with Artichokes and Mustard
Italian Rolls
Fat-Free Chocolate Frozen Yogurt with Vanilla Wafer

Quick Meal Countdown:
1. Cook angel hair pasta.
2. Prepare sole.
3. Sauté vegetables for pasta.
4. Top pasta with sautéed vegetables.
5. Before serving, top chocolate frozen yogurt with 1 cookie.

Scaloppine of Sole with Herbs
Prep Time: 15 minutes
Cook Time: 5 minutes

Ingredients:
1	garlic clove
	A few chive stalks
14	oz small sole filets
2	tsps dried oregano
5 1/2	Tbls flour
1	Tbl Bertolli® Gentile extra virgin olive oil
1/2	cup white wine
	Salt
1	(14 1/2-oz) can diced tomatoes

Directions:
Cut the garlic clove in half, and chop the chives. Wash and drain the fish filets and sprinkle them with oregano. Dip them in the flour, pressing carefully on both sides.

Heat the oil and garlic in a large pan, add the fish filets and fry them on both sides. Wet them with the wine and a little water so that the cooking juice becomes creamy, and add salt.

Add the diced tomato; continue cooking for 1 minute, add the chives and serve. Discard the garlic clove before serving.
Yield: 4 servings.

Per Serving:	185 calories, 13 g carbohydrate, 20 g protein, 4 g fat, 105 mg cholesterol, 236 mg sodium
Exchanges:	3 very lean meats, 1 vegetable, 1 fat

Angel Hair with Artichokes and Mustard

Prep Time: 20 minutes
Cook Time: 20 minutes

Ingredients:

1	clove garlic, chopped
1	Tbl olive oil
1	medium red bell pepper, cut into thin strips
1	(6 1/2-oz) jar marinated artichoke hearts, chopped, marinade reserved
1/4	cup Grey Poupon® Dijon Mustard
8	oz angel hair pasta, cooked and drained
1/4	cup cooking water reserved Grated Parmesan cheese

At The Market

1	bulb garlic
1	bunch chives
14	oz sole filets
1	medium red bell pepper
1	bag Italian rolls
1	pint fat-free chocolate frozen yogurt
1	box vanilla wafers

Per Serving: 153 calories, 24 g carbohydrate, 5 g protein, 4 g fat, 0 mg cholesterol, 454 mg sodium (without Parmesan)
Exchanges: 1 starch, 1 vegetable, 1 fat

Directions:

Cook and stir garlic in olive oil in a large skillet. Add red pepper and cook 2 minutes. Add artichokes with marinade and mustard. Add cooked pasta; toss, adding some reserved cooking water if needed. Serve with grated Parmesan cheese if desired. Yield: 4 servings.

Kitchen Staples:
• dried oregano • flour • extra-virgin olive oil • white wine • salt •
• canned, diced tomatoes • marinated artichoke hearts • Dijon mustard •
• angel hair pasta • Parmesan cheese •

Chicken Balsamic

Poultry

Italian Chicken with Broccoli and Rice

Tossed Green Salad with Fat-Free Caesar Dressing Peaches with Berry Sauce

Quick Meal Countdown:
1. Prepare Berry Sauce and chill.
2. Sauté chicken.
3. Cook rice, add broccoli to chicken.
4. Toss salad with vegetables and dressing and serve.
5. Assemble peaches and top with Berry Sauce.

Italian Chicken with Broccoli and Rice
Prep Time: 10 minutes
Cook Time: 10 minutes

Ingredients:

4	(4-oz) Tyson® IFF™ Boneless, Skinless ChickenBreasts with Rib Meat
	Salt and pepper
2	Tbls olive oil
2	cups Uncle Ben's Instant Rice
2 1/2	cups frozen broccoli florets
1	green onion, sliced
1	(14 1/2-oz) can diced tomatoes, well-drained
1/2	cup fat-free Italian salad dressing

Directions:
Sprinkle chicken lightly with salt and pepper. Heat oil in large skillet over medium-high heat. Cook, covered, 5 minutes per side. Meanwhile, cook rice according to package directions. Add broccoli to chicken in skillet; cover. Reduce heat; cook over medium heat 4 to 6 minutes or until internal juices of chicken run clear (instant-read thermometer should read 170° F when inserted in thickest part of chicken) and broccoli is at desired tenderness. Yield: 4 servings.

Serve chicken on top of rice; top with broccoli, chopped tomatoes, green onions and salad dressing.

Per Serving:	330 calories, 33 g carbohydrate, 26 g protein, 10 g fat, 51 mg cholesterol, 498 mg sodium
Exchanges:	3 very lean meats, 1 1/2 starches, 2 vegetables, 2 fats

Peaches with Berry Sauce

Prep Time: 10 minutes
Cook Time: 4 minutes

Ingredients:

1	cup hulled fresh or thawed frozen unsweetened strawberries
2	Tbls low-sugar strawberry jam
1/4	tsp ground cinnamon
4	canned juice-packed peach halves, drained
1	cup fresh or thawed unsweetened raspberries
1	tsp fresh lemon juice (optional)

At The Market

4	*(4-oz) boneless, skinless chicken breasts with rib meat*
1	*bunch green onions*
1	*bag prewashed, mixed salad greens*
1	*bag prewashed, assorted fresh vegetables*
1	*carton strawberries*
1	*carton raspberries*
1	*lemon (optional)*

Directions:

Combine strawberries and strawberry jam in a blender or food processor and purée. Strain to remove seeds; stir in cinnamon. Cover and chill. Place 1 peach half, hollow side up, on 4 individual dessert plates or in 4 glass-stemmed goblets. Spoon 3 tablespoons sauce over each half. Top with 1/4 cup raspberries. Yield: 4 servings, 1 peach half plus 3 tablespoons sauce each.

Per Serving: 71 calories, 18 g carbohydrate, 1 g protein, 0 g fat, 0 mg cholesterol, 10 mg sodium
Exchanges: 1 fruit

Kitchen Staples:

• salt • pepper • olive oil • instant rice • frozen broccoli florets •
• canned, diced tomatoes • fat-free Italian salad dressing •
• low-sugar strawberry jam • ground cinnamon • juice-packed peaches •

Oven-Fried Chicken
Mashed Potatoes with Fat-Free Gravy
Corn on the Cob
Summer Berries with Yogurt Citrus
Sauce

Quick Meal Countdown:
1. Prepare chicken and bake.
2. Boil corn.
3. Prepare mashed potatoes; heat gravy.
4. Assemble dessert.

Oven-Fried Chicken
Prep Time: 5 minutes
Cook Time: 30 minutes

Ingredients:
1   egg white
2   Tbls nonfat milk
1/2   cup dry bread crumbs
1   tsp herb blend, crushed
1/4   tsp paprika
4   (4-oz) chicken breasts, skinned
      and boneless
      Nonstick vegetable spray

Directions:
Preheat oven to 400° F. In a small bowl, beat egg white with a whisk until frothy, stir in milk. In another bowl, combine bread crumbs, herb blend and paprika, mixing well. Dip chicken in egg white/ milk mixture and coat with seasoned bread crumbs. Place on a shallow baking pan that has been coated with nonstick vegetable spray. Bake for 30 minutes or until golden brown and juices run clear when meat is pierced in its thickest part with a fork. Yield: 4 servings.

Per Serving: 185 calories, 10 g carbohydrate, 29 g protein, 2 g fat, 66 mg cholesterol, 208 mg sodium
Exchanges: 3 very lean meats, 1/2 starch

Summer Berries with Yogurt Citrus Sauce

Prep Time: 10 minutes
Cook Time: 5 minutes

Ingredients:

1	cup plain lowfat yogurt
1/4	cup honey
2	tsps lemon juice, fresh squeezed
2	tsps lime juice, fresh squeezed
1/2	tsp lemon peel, finely shredded
1/2	tsp lime peel, finely shredded
4	cups total: raspberries, blackberries, blueberries, strawberries and green grapes
8	sugar wafer cookies

Directions:

Blend first 6 ingredients. Divide fruit between 4 goblets or parfait glasses. Spoon sauce over fruit and garnish with 2 sugar wafer cookies each. Yield: 4 servings.

At The Market

1	carton eggs
1	pint nonfat milk
4	(4-oz) skinless, boneless chicken breasts
1	box instant mashed potatoes
1	(10-oz) jar fat-free gravy
4	ears corn
1	(8-oz) carton plain lowfat yogurt
1	lemon
1	lime
1	carton raspberries
1	carton blackberries
1	carton blueberries
1	carton strawberries
1	bag green grapes
1	box sugar wafer cookies

Per Serving: 199 calories, 45 g carbohydrate, 5 g protein, 2 g fat, 5 mg cholesterol, 68 mg sodium

Exchanges: 1 starch, 2 fruits

Kitchen Staples:

• dry bread crumbs • herb blend • paprika • nonstick vegetable spray • honey •

Asian Chicken

Teriyaki Snow Peas
Steamed White Rice
Fortune Cookies

Quick Meal Countdown:

1. Prepare marinade for chicken.
2. Marinate chicken.
3. Cook rice.
4. Broil chicken.
5. Prepare snow peas and top with almonds.

Asian Chicken

Prep Time: 5 minutes
Marinate Time: 15 minutes
Cook Time: 10 minutes

Ingredients:

1/4	cup soy sauce
3	Tbls orange juice
2	Tbls honey
1/8	cup vegetable oil
1/2	tsp sesame oil
1	tsp McCormick® Cilantro Leaves
1/4	tsp McCormick® Garlic Powder
1/4	tsp McCormick® Ground Ginger
1	lb boneless, skinless chicken breasts, cut into 3/4-in strips

Directions:

Place soy sauce, orange juice, honey, vegetable oil, sesame oil, cilantro, garlic and ginger in 1-cup glass measure and mix until well-combined. Pour into self-closing plastic bag. Add chicken strips and toss or stir to coat. Marinate at least 15 minutes. Preheat broiler or grill. Remove chicken from marinade and discard marinade. Weave chicken strips onto metal skewers and broil or grill 8 minutes or until chicken is cooked, turning halfway through cooking. Yield: 4 servings.

Per Serving:	151 calories, 4 g carbohydrate, 27 g protein, 3 g fat, 66 mg cholesterol, 442 mg sodium
Exchanges:	3 very lean meats, 1/2 starch

Teriyaki Snow Peas

Cook Time: 10 minutes

Ingredients:
- 1/2 (16-oz) package frozen snow peas
- 1 1/2 tsps sesame oil
- 4 Tbls teriyaki-flavored, sliced almonds

Directions:
Prepare frozen snow peas as directed on package. Stir in sesame oil. Top each serving with 1 tablespoon almonds. Yield: 4 servings.

Per Serving:	57 calories, 4 g carbohydrate, 2 g protein, 4 g fat, 0 mg cholesterol, 189 mg sodium
Exchanges:	1 vegetable, 1 fat

At The Market

- 1 (12-oz) carton orange juice
- 1 bunch fresh cilantro
- 1 lb boneless, skinless chicken breasts
- 1 (6-oz) bag teriyaki-flavored, sliced almonds
- 1 box fortune cookies

Kitchen Staples:
• soy sauce • honey • vegetable oil • sesame oil • garlic powder •
• ground ginger • frozen snow peas • instant white rice •

Chicken Balsamic
Orange Rice Pilaf
Italian Vegetable Medley
Red Pears with Green Grapes

Quick Meal Countdown:
1. Prepare rice.
2. Brown chicken.
3. Steam vegetables.
4. Complete chicken dish.
5. Prepare fruit.

Chicken Balsamic
Prep Time: 10 minutes
Cook Time: 20 minutes

Ingredients:
> Nonstick vegetable spray
> 4   (4-oz) chicken breasts, skinned and boneless
> 2   tsps extra-virgin olive oil
> 2   small cloves garlic, finely minced or pressed
> 1/2   lb fresh mushrooms, quartered
> 2 1/2 Tbls balsamic vinegar
> 1/2   cup low-sodium chicken broth
> 1/4   tsp dried thyme, crushed
> 1/8   tsp freshly ground black pepper, or to taste
> Chopped fresh parsley for garnish

Directions:
Coat a 10-inch skillet with nonstick vegetable spray. Heat over medium heat. When hot, add chicken and cook until light brown, about 3 minutes on each side. Transfer chicken to a plate. Add olive oil to pan, sauté garlic and mushrooms briefly, being careful not to burn garlic. Return chicken to pan, add vinegar, chicken broth, thyme and pepper. Reduce heat, cover and simmer for 15 minutes or until chicken is cooked. Juices will run clear when meat is pierced in its thickest part with a fork. Transfer to serving dish and top chicken with mushrooms and pan sauce. Sprinkle with chopped parsley. Yield: 4 servings.

Per Serving:	138 calories, 6 g carbohydrate, 20 g protein, 4 g fat, 43 mg cholesterol, 248 mg sodium
Exchanges:	3 very lean meats, 1 fat

Orange Rice Pilaf

Prep Time: 5 minutes
Cook Time: 25 minutes

Ingredients:

1/2	cup chopped onions
1	Tbl margarine
1	cup regular long-grain rice
1	(14 1/2-oz) can low-sodium chicken broth
1/4	cup orange juice
1/8	tsp grated orange peel
1/4	cup sliced almonds

At The Market

4	(4-oz) skinless, boneless chicken breasts
1	bulb garlic
1/2	lb mushrooms
1	bunch fresh parsley
1	onion
1	(12-oz) carton orange juice
1	orange
2	red pears
1	bunch green grapes

Directions:

In a skillet, sauté onions and rice with margarine until golden brown (3 to 5 minutes). Add remaining ingredients; heat to a boil. Reduce heat; cover and simmer 20 minutes. Yield: 6 servings.

Per Serving: 179 calories, 28 g carbohydrate, 4 g protein, 5 g fat, 0 mg cholesterol, 327 mg sodium

Exchanges: 1 1/2 starches, 1 fat

Kitchen Staples:

• nonstick vegetable spray • extra-virgin olive oil • balsamic vinegar •
• low-sodium chicken broth • dried thyme • black pepper • margarine •
• long-grain rice • sliced almonds • Italian vegetable medley •

Chicken Marinara
Pasta
Green Beans Sauté
Nonfat Cappuccino with Cinnamon

Quick Meal Countdown:
1. Prepare pasta.
2. Prepare chicken as directed.
   While marinara simmers, prepare green beans.
3. Serve chicken over fettucine.
4. Sprinkle green beans with almonds.
5. Prepare Cappuccino.

Chicken Marinara
Prep Time: 5 minutes
Cook Time: 25 minutes

Ingredients:
4	(4-oz) chicken breasts, skinned and boneless
1	tsp garlic powder
	Nonstick vegetable spray
1	tsp olive oil
1	(28-oz) can crushed tomatoes with purée
1	tsp dried basil leaves, crushed
1	tsp dried parsley flakes
1/4	tsp freshly ground black pepper

Directions:
Pound each chicken breast between plastic wrap or waxed paper with flat side of meat mallet to 1/4-inch thickness. Sprinkle chicken with 1/2 teaspoon of garlic powder. Coat a 10-inch skillet with nonstick vegetable spray. Heat olive oil over medium heat. When hot, add chicken and cook for 5 minutes until light brown. Add tomatoes, remaining 1/2 teaspoon garlic powder, basil, parsley and pepper. Reduce heat to low; cover and simmer for 20 minutes. Yield: 4 servings.

Per Serving:	199 calories, 11 g carbohydrate, 29 g protein, 4 g fat, 72 mg cholesterol, 687 mg sodium
Exchanges:	3 very lean meats, 2 vegetables, 1 fat

Green Beans Sauté

Prep Time: 5 minutes
Cook Time: 15 minutes

Ingredients:

3	cups fresh or frozen whole green beans
1/4	cup Italian salad dressing
1/4	cup Grey Poupon® Dijon Mustard
2	Tbls Planters® Sliced Almonds, toasted

At The Market

4	*(4-oz) skinless, boneless chicken breasts*
3	*cups fresh or frozen whole green beans*
1	*(4.1-oz) box instant cappuccino mix*

Directions:
Cook and stir beans in salad dressing in large skillet over medium heat to desired tenderness. Stir in mustard; heat through. Sprinkle with almonds just before serving. Yield: 4 servings.

Per Serving: 125 calories, 13 g carbohydrate, 3 g protein, 7 g fat, 4 mg cholesterol, 471 mg sodium
Exchanges: 2 vegetables, 1 fat

Kitchen Staples:
• garlic powder • nonstick vegetable spray • olive oil • canned, crushed tomatoes •
• dried basil • dried parsley • black pepper • pasta •
• Italian salad dressing • Dijon mustard • sliced almonds • cinnamon •

Cajun Turkey Burgers

Assorted Vegetables with Lowfat Ranch Dip
Baked Potato Chips
Strawberry Angel Food Cake

Quick Meal Countdown:
1. Prepare strawberry sauce and chill.
2. Grill turkey burgers.
3. Prepare sauce for burgers.
4. Right before serving, drizzle sauce on burgers and assemble cakes.

Cajun Turkey Burgers
Prep Time: 5 minutes
Cook Time: 15 minutes

Ingredients:

	Nonstick vegetable spray
1	lb ground turkey breast
1	Tbl Worcestershire sauce
2	tsps Creole seasoning, divided
1/2	(14 1/2-oz) can no-salt, stewed tomatoes, drained
1/2	tsp minced garlic
4	hamburger buns, toasted

Directions:
Spray cold grill rack with nonstick vegetable spray. Prepare charcoal grill for direct-heat cooking. In medium bowl, combine turkey, Worcestershire sauce and 1 teaspoon Creole seasoning. Evenly divide turkey mixture into 4 burgers, approximately 3 1/2 inches in diameter. Grill burgers 5 to 6 minutes per side or until 160° F is reached (using meat thermometer) and meat is no longer pink in center.

In a small saucepan, over medium-high heat, combine tomatoes, remaining Creole seasoning and garlic. Cook 5 minutes or until most of liquid has evaporated. To serve, place burger on bottom half of each bun, drizzle 3 tablespoons sauce over burger and top with other half of bun. Yield: 4 servings.

Per Serving:	337 calories, 27 g carbohydrate, 25 g protein, 14 g fat, 57 mg cholesterol, 782 mg sodium
Exchanges:	3 very lean meats, 2 starches

Strawberry Angel Food Cake

Prep Time: 5 minutes
Cook Time: 10 minutes

Ingredients:

1/4	cup water
2	tsps cornstarch
4	cups frozen unsweetened strawberries, thawed
2	tsps honey
1/2	loaf angel food cake

Directions:

Mix water and cornstarch. In a small saucepan, blend strawberries and cornstarch mixture. Add honey. Bring to a simmer over medium heat, stirring constantly. Remove from heat and cool completely. To serve, slice cake into 6 equal pieces. Lay cake slices on 6 individual dessert plates. Drizzle 1/3 cup strawberry sauce over each slice. Yield: 6 servings.

Per Serving:	118 calories, 28 g carbohydrate, 2 g protein, 0 g fat, 0 mg cholesterol, 215 mg sodium
Exchanges:	1 starch, 1 fruit

At The Market

1	lb ground turkey breast
1	bulb garlic
4	hamburger buns
1	bag prewashed, assorted, precut fresh vegetables
1	(16-oz) carton lowfat ranch dip
1	(13 1/2-oz) bag baked potato chips
1	(16-oz) loaf angel food cake

Kitchen Staples:

• nonstick vegetable spray • Worcestershire sauce • Creole seasoning •
• canned, no-salt, stewed tomatoes • cornstarch •
• frozen, unsweetened strawberries • honey •

Burgundy Turkey Cutlets

Brown and Wild Rice with Pecans
Green Beans with Tarragon
Apple Crisp

Quick Meal Countdown:
1. Prepare Apple Crisp and bake.
2. Prepare boxed rice mix.
3. Steam green beans.
4. Prepare turkey cutlets.
5. Just before serving, sprinkle rice with pecans and green beans with tarragon.

Burgundy Turkey Cutlets
Prep Time: 5 minutes
Cook Time: 10 minutes

Ingredients:
- 1/4 cup dry red wine
- 1 Tbl Dijon mustard
- 1 Tbl honey
- Nonstick vegetable spray
- 1 lb turkey breast cutlets, pounded to an even thickness
- 1/2 tsp garlic, minced
- Salt
- Pepper

Directions:
In a small bowl, combine wine, mustard and honey; set aside. In a large, nonstick skillet coated with nonstick vegetable spray, over medium-high heat, sauté turkey 2 to 3 minutes per side or until no longer pink in center. Transfer turkey to platter and keep warm. In same skillet, over medium heat, sauté garlic 30 seconds. Add wine mixture and heat 2 to 3 minutes until thickened, stirring constantly. To serve, drizzle sauce over turkey. Yield: 4 servings.

Per Serving:	160 calories, 5 g carbohydrate, 21 g protein, 1 g fat, 70 mg cholesterol, 169 mg sodium
Exchanges:	3 very lean meats

Apple Crisp

Prep Time: 10 minutes
Cook Time: 20 minutes

Ingredients:

2	apples
	Nonstick vegetable spray
1	cup oatmeal
1/2	cup whole-wheat flour
1/2	cup packed brown sugar
1/2	tsp cinnamon
1/4	cup margarine, softened

Directions:

Preheat oven to 350° F. Cut apples into small wedges. Layer wedges on bottom of 8 x 8-inch pan coated with nonstick vegetable spray. Mix dry ingredients. Add margarine with a fork, stir until mixture resembles coarse crumbs. Sprinkle dry mixture over apples. Bake 20 minutes or until golden brown. Yield: 6 servings.

At The Market

1	lb turkey breast cutlets
1	bulb garlic
1	lb green beans
2	apples

Per Serving: 250 calories, 41 g carbohydrate, 4 g protein, 9 g fat, 0 mg cholesterol, 97 mg sodium

Exchanges: 2 starches, 1/2 fruit, 2 fats

Kitchen Staples:

• dry red wine • Dijon mustard • honey • nonstick vegetable spray • salt •
• pepper • brown and wild rice • pecans • tarragon •
• oatmeal • whole-wheat flour •
• brown sugar • cinnamon • margarine •

British Isles T-Bone Steak

Meats

British Isles T-Bone Steak

Grilled Rosemary Corn on the Cob
Sliced Tomatoes with Fat-Free Blue Cheese Dressing
Watermelon

Directions:
Mix steak sauce, mustards and vinegar; set aside. Grill or broil steaks for 7 to 9 minutes on each side or until desired doneness, brushing with steak sauce mixture occasionally. Yield: 4 servings.

Quick Meal Countdown:
1. Prepare steak sauce and mixture for corn.
2. Grill steaks and corn.
3. Slice tomatoes and top with dressing.
4. Cut watermelon and serve.

Per Serving:	224 calories, 4 g carbohydrate, 17 g protein, 16 g fat, 53 mg cholesterol, 371 mg sodium
Exchanges:	3 lean meats

British Isles T-Bone Steak
Prep Time: 5 minutes
Cook Time: 14 minutes

Ingredients:

1/3	cup A-1® Steak Sauce
2	Tbls Grey Poupon® Dijon Mustard
2	tsps dry mustard
2	Tbls malt or cider vinegar
1	(1-lb) beef loin T-bone steak, 1-in thick

Grilled Rosemary
Corn on the Cob

Prep Time: 15 minutes
Cook Time: 15 minutes

Ingredients:

2   Tbls reduced fat margarine, melted
1/4 cup fresh lemon juice
1/4 tsp dried rosemary
4   (5-oz) ears of corn

Directions:

Mix margarine, lemon juice and rosemary in
small bowl. Peel back husks from corn and
remove silk. Brush with lemon mixture.
Replace husks. Grill over low heat for 15
minutes, turning frequently for even cooking. Yield: 4 servings.

Per Serving: 106 calories, 19 g carbohydrate, 3 g
protein, 4 g fat, 0 mg cholesterol,
81 mg sodium
Exchanges: 1 starch, 1 fat

At The Market

1   (1-lb) T-bone steak
1   lemon
4   (5-oz) ears of corn
4   medium tomatoes
1   watermelon

Kitchen Staples:
• steak sauce • Dijon mustard • dry mustard • malt or cider vinegar •
• reduced fat margarine • dried rosemary • fat-free blue cheese dressing •

Thai-Style Steak Pizza

Tossed Green Salad with Fat-Free Vinaigrette
Fudgey Brownies

Quick Meal Countdown:

1. Prepare and bake brownies.
2. Stir-fry steak.
3. Assemble pizza and bake.
4. Toss salad with vinaigrette.

Thai-Style Steak Pizza
Prep Time: 6 minutes
Cook Time: 13 minutes

Ingredients:

1 1/4 lbs boneless beef top sirloin steak, cut 1-in thick
1 Tbl roasted garlic oil
1/4 cup sliced green onions
1 (10-oz) package prebaked, thin pizza crust (12-in diameter)
3 Tbls prepared Thai peanut sauce
1 1/2 cups (6 oz) shredded pizza cheese blend
1/2 cup packaged shredded carrots
2 Tbls chopped fresh cilantro

Directions:

Preheat oven to 425° F. Cut steak lengthwise in half, then crosswise into 1/4-inch-thick strips. In large, nonstick skillet, heat garlic oil over medium-high heat until hot. Stir-fry steak and onions in 2 batches, 2 to 3 minutes each, or until outside surface of steak is no longer pink. Remove from skillet with slotted spoon.

Place pizza crust onto ungreased, large baking sheet. Spread with peanut sauce; sprinkle with 1/2 cup of cheese. Top with steak mixture; sprinkle with remaining 1 cup of cheese. Bake in 425° F oven 11 to 13 minutes or until cheese is melted. Sprinkle with carrots and cilantro. Cut into 8 wedges. Serve immediately. Yield: 8 servings.

Per Serving: 266 calories, 18 g carbohydrate, 23 g protein, 11 g fat, 53 mg cholesterol, 429 mg sodium
Exchanges: 3 lean meats, 1 starch, 1 vegetable

Fudgey Brownies

Prep Time: 5 minutes
Cook Time: 25 minutes

Ingredients:

1   (19-oz) box plain brownie mix
2   egg whites
1/2 cup plain nonfat yogurt
     Water (amount specified on
     brownie mix box)
     Nonstick vegetable spray

Directions:

Preheat oven to 350° F. Prepare brownies as
directed on box, substituting egg whites for
eggs and nonfat yogurt for oil. Add water.
Blend. Spread batter into 11 3/4 x 7 1/2-inch
baking pan coated with nonstick vegetable
spray on bottom only. Bake 25 minutes or
until edges begin to pull away from sides of
pan. Cool completely. Cut into bars.
Yield: 16 servings.

At The Market

1 1/4 lbs boneless beef top sirloin steak
1   bunch green onions
1   (10-oz) package prebaked, thin
     pizza crust
1   bottle Thai peanut sauce
1   (6-oz) package shredded pizza
     cheese
1   (10-oz) package shredded carrots
1   bunch fresh cilantro
1   bag prewashed, mixed salad
     greens
1   bag prewashed, assorted fresh
     vegetables

1   (19-oz) box plain brownie mix
1   carton eggs
1   (8-oz) carton plain nonfat yogurt

Per Serving: 153 calories, 26 g carbohydrate, 2 g
                protein, 5 g fat, 0 mg cholesterol,
                115 mg sodium
Exchanges: 1 1/2 starches, 1 fat

Kitchen Staples:
• roasted garlic oil • fat-free vinaigrette • nonstick vegetable spray •

Beef Kabobs with Parmesan Orzo

Chilled Vegetables Oregano
Italian Rolls
Lemon Sorbet

Quick Meal Countdown:
1. Prepare vegetables and chill.
2. Marinate beef.
3. Cook orzo.
4. Grill beef. Serve on orzo.

Beef Kabobs with Parmesan Orzo
Prep Time: 10 minutes
Cook Time: 10 minutes

Ingredients:
Beef Kabobs:

1	lb boneless beef top sirloin steak, cut 1-in thick
1	Tbl chopped fresh basil
1	Tbl prepared Italian salad dressing
2	large cloves garlic, minced
2	red or yellow bell peppers, cut into 1-in pieces

Parmesan Orzo:

1	cup uncooked orzo pasta
2-3	Tbls chopped fresh basil
2	Tbls shredded Parmesan cheese
2	tsps olive oil

Directions:
Soak eight 8-inch bamboo skewers in water 10 minutes; drain. Cut beef into 1-inch pieces. Combine 1 tablespoon basil, dressing and garlic in large bowl. Add beef and bell peppers; toss to coat. Cook orzo as directed on package; drain. Toss with basil, cheese and oil. Keep warm. Alternately thread beef and peppers evenly onto bamboo skewers. Place on grill over medium, ash-covered coals. Grill, uncovered, 8 to 10 minutes for medium-rare to medium doneness, turning occasionally. Serve on orzo. Yield: 4 servings.

Per Serving:	381 calories, 35 g carbohydrate, 33 g protein, 12 g fat, 70 mg cholesterol, 135 mg sodium
Exchanges:	3 lean meats, 2 starches, 1 vegetable, 1 fat

Chilled Vegetables Oregano

Prep Time: 10 minutes
Cook Time: 10 minutes
Marinate Time: 24 hours

Ingredients:
1	cup cauliflower
1	cup broccoli
1	cup carrots, sliced 1/4-in thick
3/4	cup white wine vinegar
1/2	cup water
1	clove garlic, sliced
1	tsp red pepper flakes
1	Tbl oregano leaves, crushed

Directions:
Rinse the cauliflower and broccoli and cut into florets. Combine the cauliflower and broccoli with the remaining ingredients in a saucepan. Bring to a boil, cover, reduce heat and simmer 10 minutes, or until vegetables are at desired tenderness. Transfer the mixture to a ceramic or glass bowl. Cover and chill. Drain well and serve. Yield: 4 servings.

At The Market
1	lb boneless beef top sirloin
1	bunch basil
1	bulb garlic
2	red or yellow bell peppers
1	box orzo pasta
1	head cauliflower
1	bunch broccoli
1	bag carrots
1	bag Italian rolls

Per Serving: 47 calories, 7 g carbohydrate, 2 g protein, 0 g fat, 0 mg cholesterol, 28 mg sodium
Exchanges: 2 vegetables

Kitchen Staples:
• Italian salad dressing • Parmesan cheese • olive oil • white wine vinegar •
• red pepper flakes • dried oregano • lemon sorbet •

Confetti Beef Tacos
Spanish Rice
Baked Tomatoes
Papaya with Lime

Quick Meal Countdown:
1. Prepare beef.
2. Prepare rice.
3. Prepare and bake tomatoes.
4. Heat taco shells.
5. Assemble tacos and garnish papayas withlime wheels.

Confetti Beef Tacos
Prep Time: 10 minutes
Cook Time: 10 minutes

Ingredients:
4	packaged taco shells
1/4	lb lean (7% fat) ground beef
1/2	tsp chili powder
	Dash salt
1/4	cup salsa
1/4	(11-oz) can corn, drained
	Shredded lettuce, reduced fat cheddar cheese, chopped tomatoes

Directions:
Preheat oven to 350° F. Brown ground beef over medium-high heat until thoroughly cooked; drain. Stir in chili powder, salt, salsa and corn; heat. Heat taco shells as directed on package. Spoon beef filling into shells; top with 1 tablespoon each lettuce, cheese and tomatoes. Yield: 4 servings.

Per Serving:	157 calories, 12 g carbohydrate, 7 g protein, 9 g fat, 21 mg cholesterol, 286 mg sodium
Exchanges:	1 lean meat, 1 starch, 1 fat

Baked Tomatoes

Prep Time: 10 minutes
Cook Time: 20 minutes

Ingredients:

   Nonstick vegetable spray
2 fresh tomatoes cut in halves
1 Tbl olive oil
1/2 tsp chopped fresh parsley or
   1 tsp dried parsley flakes
1 tsp dried oregano
1 tsp dried basil

Directions:

Preheat oven to 350° F. Lightly spray a 9 x 9-inch baking dish with nonstick vegetable spray. Place tomato halves in baking dish, cut side up. Drizzle oil over tomatoes. Sprinkle remaining ingredients on top and bake 20 minutes. Serve hot. Yield: 4 servings.

Per Serving: 44 calories, 3 g carbohydrate,
         1 g protein, 4 g fat, 0 mg cholesterol,
         6 mg sodium
Exchanges: 1 vegetable, 1 fat

At The Market

1   package taco shells
1/4 lb lean ground beef
1   head lettuce
1   package reduced fat cheddar cheese
3   tomatoes
1   bunch fresh parsley or 1 bottle
    dried parsley
2   papayas
1   lime

Kitchen Staples:
• chili powder • salt • salsa • canned corn • boxed Spanish rice •
• nonstick vegetable spray • olive oil • dried oregano • dried basil •

Orange Mustard Pork Chop Skillet
Fruited Couscous
Asparagus with Lemon

Ingredients:

4	(4-oz) top loin pork chops
1/3	cup orange juice
3	Tbls soy sauce
2	Tbls honey mustard

Quick Meal Countdown:
1. Prepare pork chops.
2. While pork chops simmer, microwave asparagus.
3. Prepare couscous.
4. Squeeze lemon juice onto asparagus and garnish couscous with green onions.

Directions:

In a nonstick skillet, brown pork chops on one side over medium-high heat; turn; stir in remaining ingredients. On low heat, simmer covered for 6 to 8 minutes. Yield: 4 servings.

Orange Mustard Pork Chop Skillet
Prep Time: 5 minutes
Cook Time: 10 minutes

Per Serving:	200 calories, 0 g carbohydrate, 26 g protein, 7 g fat, 60 mg cholesterol, 370 mg sodium
Exchanges:	4 lean meats

Fruited Couscous

Cook Time: 5 minutes

Ingredients:
1   (10-oz) box couscous
2   cups water
1   Tbl olive oil
1/4 cup pine nuts
1/2 cup fresh raspberries
2   green onions, diced

At The Market

4   (4-oz) top loin pork chops
1   (12-oz) carton orange juice
1   (4-oz) bag pine nuts
1   carton raspberries
1   bunch green onions
1   bunch asparagus
1   lemon

Directions:
Prepare couscous as directed on package.
Stir in pine nuts and raspberries. Garnish
with green onions. Yield: 6 servings.

Per Serving: 239 calories, 39 g carbohydrate,
8 g protein, 5 g fat, 0 mg cholesterol,
5 mg sodium
Exchanges: 2 starches, 1 fat

Kitchen Staples:
• soy sauce • honey mustard • couscous • olive oil •

Southwestern Grilled Pork Tenderloin
Prep Time: 15 minutes
Cook Time: 15-20 minutes

Ingredients:

2	whole pork tenderloins (1 1/2 lbs)
5	tsps chili powder
1 1/2	tsps dried oregano
3/4	tsp ground cumin
2	garlic cloves, crushed
1	Tbl vegetable oil

Directions:

In a small bowl, mix all ingredients together except pork. Rub mixture over all surfaces of pork. Cover and refrigerate 10 minutes. Grill over medium-hot fire, turning occasionally, for 15 to 20 minutes, until meat thermometer inserted reads 155-160° F. Slice to serve. Yield: 6 servings.

Per Serving:	170 calories, 3 g carbohydrate, 24 g protein, 7 g fat, 75 mg cholesterol, 80 mg sodium
Exchanges:	3 lean meats

Southwestern Grilled Pork Tenderloin

Fat-Free Flour Tortillas
Spinach Spring Salad with Vinaigrette
Grilled Pineapple

Quick Meal Countdown:

1. Rub pork with seasoning and refrigerate.
2. Prepare vinaigrette.
3. Grill pork as directed. Grill pineapple 5 minutes per side.
4. Toss salad and serve with tortillas.

Spinach Spring Salad with Vinaigrette

Prep Time: 5 minutes
Cook Time: 10 minutes

Ingredients:

Vinaigrette:

1/4	cup fresh lemon juice
1/4	cup red wine vinegar
1	tsp dried thyme, crushed
2	tsps extra-virgin olive oil
2	garlic cloves, finely minced or pressed
1 1/2	Tbls Dijon mustard

Salad:

1	lb fresh asparagus spears
1/4	lb fresh mushrooms, sliced
1	bunch fresh spinach, stems removed, leaves torn into bite-sized pieces
1/2	head red leaf lettuce, torn into bite-sized pieces
1/4	head red cabbage, shredded
3	green onions, thinly sliced

Directions:

For the vinaigrette, combine all ingredients, except mustard, in a small saucepan. Cook over medium heat for 3 to 4 minutes, or until thoroughly heated. Add mustard; whisk until well-blended. Serve warm.

At The Market

1 1/2	lbs pork tenderloin
1	bulb garlic
1	package fat-free flour tortillas (7-8 in)
1	lemon
1	lb asparagus
1	(8-oz) carton mushrooms
1	bunch spinach
1	head red leaf lettuce
1	head red cabbage
1	bunch green onions
1	pineapple

For the salad, snap the ends off the asparagus; discard ends. Cut spears into 2-inch pieces, and steam for 4 to 5 minutes, or until at desired tenderness. Rinse in ice water and drain. Combine asparagus, mushrooms, spinach, lettuce, cabbage and green onions in a large bowl and toss. Pour warm vinaigrette over the salad and toss gently. Yield: 6 servings.

Per Serving:	62 calories, 10 g carbohydrate, 4 g protein, 2 g fat, 0 mg cholesterol, 125 mg sodium
Exchanges:	2 vegetables

Kitchen Staples:

• chili powder • dried oregano • ground cumin • vegetable oil •
• red wine vinegar • dried thyme • extra-virgin olive oil • Dijon mustard •

Mediterranean Lamb Shish Kabobs
Wheat Pilaf
Steamed Green Beans with Feta Cheese
Savory Fresh Apricot Bites

Quick Meal Countdown:
1. Prepare Wheat Pilaf.
2. Prepare marinade and marinate lamb.
3. Broil lamb kabobs.
4. Steam green beans.
5. Just before serving, top beans with feta cheese and assemble Apricot Bites.

Mediterranean Lamb Shish Kabobs
Prep Time: 5 minutes
Marinate Time: 20 minutes
Cook Time: 10 minutes

Ingredients:
3/4	cup plain nonfat yogurt
1/4	tsp hot pepper sauce
2	large garlic cloves, finely minced or pressed
1/2	cup fresh lemon juice
1/4	cup minced fresh mint leaves
1/4	tsp paprika
1	lb loin of lamb, cut into 1-in cubes

Directions:
Combine all ingredients except lamb in a medium, nonaluminum bowl; mix well. Add cubed lamb, turning to coat well with marinade. Place in a shallow glass or ceramic pan and pierce meat with a fork. Cover the pan with plastic wrap and marinate in refrigerator for 20 minutes. Divide lamb into 4 equal portions and thread on skewers. Broil 3 to 4 inches from heat for 10 minutes, turning once. Yield: 4 servings.

Per Serving: 274 calories, 7 g carbohydrate, 24 g protein, 16 g fat, 78 mg cholesterol, 114 mg sodium
Exchanges: 3 lean meats, 1 fat

Savory Fresh Apricot Bites

Prep Time: 5 minutes

Ingredients:
- 1   oz fat-free cream cheese, softened
- 4   fresh apricots, halved
- 2   Tbls pistachios, finely chopped

Directions:
Stir cream cheese until smooth; pipe or spoon into apricot halves. Sprinkle tops with pistachios. Serve as an appetizer, snack or dessert. Yield: 4 servings.

Per Serving: 43 calories, 5 g carbohydrate, 2 g protein, 2 g fat, 1 mg cholesterol, 67 mg sodium
Exchanges: 1/2 fruit

At The Market

- 1   *(8-oz) carton plain nonfat yogurt*
- 1   *bulb garlic*
- 1   *lemon*
- 1   *bunch fresh mint*
- 1   *lb loin of lamb*
- 1   *lb green beans*
- 4   *fresh apricots*

Kitchen Staples:
• hot pepper sauce • paprika • wheat pilaf mix • reduced fat feta cheese • fat-free cream cheese • pistachios •

Linguini with Mushroom Marinara

Meatless Mains

Roasted Garlic and Spinach Tortellini

Mixed Greens with Poppy Seed Vinaigrette
Breadsticks
Melon Medley

Quick Meal Countdown:
1. Defrost Melon Medley.
2. Prepare Poppy Seed Vinaigrette.
3. Cook Roasted Garlic and Spinach Tortellini.
4. Before serving, toss salad.

Roasted Garlic and Spinach Tortellini
Prep Time: 5 minutes
Cook Time: 10 minutes

Ingredients:
1   (10-oz) package frozen chopped spinach, thawed
2   Tbls McCormick® Monterey Style Spice Blends
1/2 cup grated Parmesan cheese
1   cup nonfat milk
16 oz cheese tortellini, cooked and drained

Directions:
Heat spinach and Spice Blends in saucepan until water evaporates. Stir in cheese, milk and tortellini. Cook and stir 3 to 5 minutes. Yield: 5 servings.

Per Serving:	373 calories, 49 g carbohydrate, 22 g protein, 11 g fat, 60 mg cholesterol, 903 mg sodium
Exchanges:	2 lean meats, 2 1/2 starches, 1 vegetable, 1 fat

Poppy Seed Vinaigrette

Prep Time: 10 minutes

Ingredients:

1/2	cup orange juice
1/3	cup red wine vinegar
1/4	cup Grey Poupon® Dijon Mustard
2	Tbls olive oil
1	Tbl poppy seeds

Directions:

Whisk together orange juice, vinegar, mustard, oil and poppy seeds in small bowl. Serve immediately or cover and store in refrigerator for up to 1 week. Yield: 10 servings.

Per Serving: 23 calories, 1 g carbohydrate, 0 g protein, 2 g fat, 0 mg cholesterol, 73 mg sodium

Exchanges: Free

At The Market

1	pint nonfat milk
1	(16-oz) package refrigerated cheese tortellini
1	bag prewashed, mixed salad greens
1	bag prewashed, assorted fresh vegetables
1	(12-oz) carton orange juice
1	(4-oz) package breadsticks

Kitchen Staples:

• frozen spinach • spice blend • Parmesan cheese • red wine vinegar •
• Dijon mustard • olive oil • poppy seeds • frozen assorted melon medley •

Jamaican Beans and Rice

Tossed Green Salad with Fat-Free Vinaigrette
Banana Cream Rum Pudding

Quick Meal Countdown:
1. Prepare pudding and chill.
2. Cook rice, keep warm.
3. Prepare Jamaican Beans.
4. Toss salad.
5 Serve stew over rice.

Jamaican Beans and Rice
Prep Time: 15 minutes
Cook Time: 15 minutes

Ingredients:

1	cup chopped onion
1/2	cup chopped red bell pepper
1/2	cup chopped green bell pepper
1	Tbl finely chopped ginger root
1 1/2	tsps minced garlic
1	small jalapeño chili, seeded and finely chopped
1	tsp dried thyme leaves
1/8	tsp ground allspice
	Nonstick vegetable spray
3	Tbls flour
1	(14-oz) can light coconut milk
1	Tbl fresh lime juice
2	tsps grated lime rind
2	cups cubed and peeled sweet potatoes (1-in cubes)
2	cups cubed and peeled yellow squash (1-in cubes)
1	(15-oz) can red beans, rinsed and drained
1	(8 1/2-oz) can baby lima beans, rinsed and drained
	Salt and pepper, to taste
2	cups instant cooked rice, hot
2	Tbls finely chopped cilantro, as garnish

Directions:
Sauté onion, bell peppers, ginger root, garlic, jalapeño chili and herbs in large saucepan coated with nonstick vegetable spray until tender, about 5 minutes. Stir in flour, cook 1 minute. Stir coconut milk, lime juice and rind into pan; add sweet potatoes and squash and heat to boiling. Reduce heat and simmer, covered, until vegetables are tender, 10 to 15 minutes. Add beans; cook until hot, 1 to 2 minutes. Season to taste with salt and pepper. Serve stew over rice; sprinkle with cilantro. Yield: 6 servings.

Per Serving:	350 calories, 57 g carbohydrate, 9 g protein, 9 g fat, 0 mg cholesterol, 361 mg sodium
Exchanges:	3 starches, 1 very lean meat, 2 vegetables, 2 fats

Banana Cream Rum Pudding

PrepTime: 10 minutes
ChillTime: 1 hour

Ingredients:
1   (3.4-oz) package SugarFree ROYAL®
     Instant Banana Cream Pudding &
     Pie Filling
2   cups 2% lowfat milk
1/2   tsp rum extract
1   large banana, sliced
1/3   cup seedless raisins
4   squares HONEY MAID® Honey
     Grahams, halved
     Ground cinnamon, for garnish

Directions:
Prepare pudding as directed on package using milk and rum extract; refrigerate. Stir in banana slices and raisins. Spoon into cups; garnish with two graham cracker pieces and cinnamon. Yield: 4 servings.

At The Market

1   onion
1   red bell pepper
1   green bell pepper
1   fresh ginger root
1   bulb garlic
1   jalapeño chili
1   (14-oz) can light coconut milk
1   lime
1   lb sweet potatoes
1   lb yellow squash
1   bunch fresh cilantro
1   bag prewashed iceburg lettuce
1   bag prewashed, assorted fresh
    vegetables
1   pint 2% lowfat milk
1   banana

Per Serving: 240 calories, 51 g carbohydrate, 6 g protein, 2 g fat, 5 mg cholesterol, 418 mg sodium
Exchanges: 2 starches, 1 fruit

Kitchen Staples:
• dried thyme • ground allspice • nonstick vegetable spray • flour •
• canned red beans • canned baby lima beans • salt • pepper • instant rice •
• fat-free vinaigrette • sugar-free, instant banana pudding • rum extract •
• raisins • graham crackers • ground cinnamon •

Linguini with Mushroom Marinara

Broiled Zucchini Halves with Parmesan
Crusty Bread
Applesauce Cheesecake

Quick Meal Countdown:
1. Prepare cheesecake and chill.
2. Prepare sauce, simmer.
3. Cook pasta, microwave zucchini.
4. Broil zucchini with Parmesan.
5. Toss pasta with sauce, and top with Parmesan.

Linguini with Mushroom Marinara
Prep Time: 10 minutes
Cook Time: 20 minutes

Ingredients:
4	cloves garlic, peeled and minced
8	oz fresh sliced mushrooms
3	Tbls olive oil
2	(14 1/2-oz) cans Italian-style chopped tomatoes, drained
12	oz linguini (or other thin pasta)
1	bunch fresh basil leaves, no stems, chopped
12	Tbls Parmesan cheese, freshly grated

Directions:
Sauté garlic and mushrooms in olive oil until golden, but not brown. Add tomatoes, and simmer over medium heat for 20 minutes. Meanwhile, prepare pasta according to package. When sauce is done simmering, remove from heat and stir in basil. Toss pasta with sauce, top with cheese.
Yield: 6 servings.

Per Serving: 344 calories, 49 g carbohydrate, 13 g protein, 11 g fat, 8 mg cholesterol, 201 mg sodium
Exchanges: 1 lean meat, 2 starches, 2 vegetables, 1 fat

Applesauce Cheesecake

Prep Time: 15 minutes
Chill Time: 1 hour

Ingredients:
- 1 (8-oz) package ROYAL® No Bake Lite Cheesecake
- 1/4 cup margarine, melted
- 1 cup 1% lowfat milk
- 1/2 cup unsweetened applesauce
- 1/2 tsp ground cinnamon

Directions:
Remove graham cracker mix from cheese-cake package. Combine graham cracker mix and margarine. Press crumb mixture on bottom and sides of 8- or 9-inch pie plate. Refrigerate. Mix milk, applesauce and cinna-mon in small bowl; add cheesecake filling. Mix as directed on package. Spread into pre-pared crust; refrigerate 1 hour. Garnish as desired. Yield: 6 servings.

At The Market

1	*bulb garlic*
1	*(8-oz) package fresh mushrooms*
1	*bunch fresh basil*
3	*zucchini*
1	*loaf French/Italian bread*
1	*(8-oz) package no-bake, light cheesecake mix*
1	*pint 1% lowfat milk*

Per Serving: 211 calories, 31 g carbohydrate, 7 g protein, 6 g fat, 13 mg cholesterol, 293 mg sodium

Exchanges: 2 starches, 1 fat

Kitchen Staples:
• olive oil • canned, Italian-style tomatoes • linguini • Parmesan cheese •
• margarine • unsweetened applesauce • ground cinnamon •

Chunky Vegetable Soup

Soups

Chunky Vegetable Soup

Chopped Salad with Swiss Cheese and Fat-Free Caesar Dressing
Apple Bran Muffins

Quick Meal Countdown:
1. Mix muffin batter and bake.
2. Prepare soup and simmer.
3. Toss salad.

Chunky Vegetable Soup
Prep Time: 10 minutes
Cook Time: 20 minutes

Ingredients:

4	(14 1/2-oz) cans low-sodium chicken broth
1/2	cup chopped red bell pepper
2	cloves garlic, minced
1	cup sliced carrots
1	cup sliced celery
1	cup sliced onion
1	tsp dried basil leaves
1/4	tsp ground black pepper
1	cup uncooked spiral macaroni
1/2	cup frozen corn

Directions:

Heat chicken broth, red pepper, garlic, carrots, celery, onion, basil and black pepper in large saucepan over medium-high heat to a boil. Stir in macaroni; simmer 10 minutes. Stir in corn; cook 5 minutes more or until macaroni is done. Yield: 8 servings.

Per Serving:	161 calories, 31 g carbohydrate, 7 g protein, 1 g fat, 1 mg cholesterol, 369 mg sodium
Exchanges:	1 1/2 starches, 1 vegetable

Apple Bran Muffins

Prep Time: 10 minutes
Chill Time: 20 minutes

Ingredients:

1	(7-oz) box bran muffin mix
1	cup applesauce
2	egg whites
1	tsp McCormick® Ground Cinnamon
1	tsp McCormick® Pure Vanilla Extract

Directions:

Grease 10 cups of 12-cup muffin pan or line with paper baking cups and set aside. Place all ingredients in medium-sized bowl and stir until well-combined. Spoon batter into 10 prepared muffin cups, filling cups no more than two-thirds full. Half-fill 2 empty cups with water. Bake in preheated, 400° F oven for 15 to 20 minutes or until toothpick inserted in center of muffin comes out clean. Remove from pan immediately and serve hot. Yield: 10 servings.

At The Market

1	red bell pepper
1	bulb garlic
1	bag carrots
1	bunch celery
1	onion
1	bunch romaine lettuce
1	bag prewashed, assorted fresh vegetables
1	(8-oz) package reduced fat Swiss cheese
1	(7-oz) box bran muffin mix
1	carton eggs

Per Serving: 103 calories, 19 g carbohydrate, 3 g protein, 2 g fat, 0 mg cholesterol, 198 mg sodium

Exchanges: 1 starch, 1/2 fruit

Kitchen Staples:

• low-sodium chicken broth • dried basil • black pepper • spiral macaroni •
• frozen corn • fat-free Caesar dressing • applesauce •
• ground cinnamon • vanilla extract •

Corn-Clam Chowder

Spinach Salad with Fat-Free Vinaigrette
Oyster Crackers
Cranberry Pecan Bars

Quick Meal Countdown:
1. Prepare soup and simmer 20-25 minutes.
2. Prepare cranberry bars and bake.
3. Toss salad.

Corn-Clam Chowder
Prep Time: 5 minutes
Cook Time: 25 minutes

Ingredients:

	Nonstick vegetable spray
1/4	cup chopped green onions
2	cups nonfat milk
2	Tbls flour
2	(6-oz) cans chopped clams, drained, juice reserved
1	(6-oz) potato, diced into 1/2-in cubes
1	(8-oz) can no-salt-added corn, drained
1/4	tsp dried thyme, crushed
1	large bay leaf
1/8	tsp cayenne pepper

Directions:
In a medium pan coated with nonstick vegetable spray, sauté green onions over medium heat until limp. Add water if necessary to keep from sticking. Mix milk with flour and add to onions. Bring to a boil, stirring constantly. Cook for 5 minutes or until mixture starts to thicken. Add reserved clam juice, potato, corn, thyme, bay leaf and cayenne pepper. Reduce heat; simmer 15 minutes or until potatoes are tender. Remove bay leaf and discard. Stir in clams and heat through. Yield: 4 servings.

Per Serving:	257 calories, 27 g carbohydrate, 28 g protein, 2 g fat, 59 mg cholesterol, 315 mg sodium
Exchanges:	3 very lean meats, 1 1/2 starches, 1/2 milk

Cranberry Pecan Bars

Prep Time: 10 minutes
Cook Time: 25 minutes

Ingredients:

1	cup margarine
1	cup all-purpose flour
1/2	cup packed brown sugar
1	tsp finely grated orange peel
1/2	cup fresh orange juice
1	egg
1/2	tsp baking powder
1/4	tsp baking soda
1/2	cup chopped pecans
1/2	cup dried cranberries
	Powdered sugar

Directions:

Preheat oven to 350° F. In a mixing bowl, beat margarine with electric mixer on medium speed for 30 seconds. Add about half the flour, brown sugar, orange peel, half the orange juice, egg, baking powder and baking soda. Beat until thoroughly combined. Beat in remaining flour and orange juice. Stir in pecans and cranberries.

At The Market

1	bunch green onions
1	pint nonfat milk
1	(6-oz) potato
1	bag prewashed spinach
1	bag prewashed, assorted fresh vegetables
1	(10-oz) box oyster crackers
1	orange
1	carton eggs
1	(12-oz) bag dried cranberries

Spread into ungreased 11 x 7 x 1 1/2-inch baking pan. Bake at 350° F for about 25 minutes or until a toothpick inserted near the center comes out clean. Cool in pan on a wire rack. Sift powdered sugar over the top. Cut into bars. Yield: 24 servings.

Per Serving: 75 calories, 10 g carbohydrate, 1 g protein, 4 g fat, 9 mg cholesterol, 48 mg sodium
Exchanges: 1 starch

Kitchen Staples:

• nonstick vegetable spray • flour • canned clams • canned, no-salt-added corn •
• dried thyme • bay leaf • cayenne pepper • fat-free vinaigrette • margarine •
• brown sugar • baking powder • baking soda • pecans • powdered sugar •

20-Minute White Bean Chili

Corn Bread
Mixed Salad with Raspberry Honey Dijon Dressing
Orange Wedges

Quick Meal Countdown:
1. Prepare salad dressing.
2. Cook chili and simmer.
3. Bake corn bread.
4. Toss salad and slice oranges.

20-Minute White Bean Chili
Prep Time: 10 minutes
Cook Time: 20 minutes

Ingredients:
1   cup chopped onion
1   clove garlic, minced
1   Tbl vegetable oil
1   lb ground turkey
1   cup chicken broth
1   (14 1/2-oz) can stewed tomatoes
1/3 cup Grey Poupon® Dijon Mustard
1   Tbl chili powder
1/8 to 1/4 tsp ground red pepper
1   (15-oz) can cannellini beans, drained and rinsed
1   (8-oz) can corn, drained

Directions:
Cook and stir onions and garlic in oil in 3-quart saucepan over medium-high heat until tender. Add turkey; cook until done, stirring occasionally to break up meat. Drain. Stir in chicken broth, tomatoes, mustard, chili powder and pepper. Heat to a boil; reduce heat. Simmer for 10 minutes. Stir in beans and corn; cook for 5 minutes. Yield: 6 servings.

Per Serving:	293 calories, 33 g carbohydrate, 26 g protein, 6 g fat, 50 mg cholesterol, 752 mg sodium
Exchanges:	3 medium-fat meats, 1 1/2 starches, 1 vegetable

Mixed Salad with Raspberry Honey Dijon Dressing

Prep Time: 5 minutes
Chill Time: 20 minutes

Ingredients:

1/3	cup Grey Poupon® Country Dijon Mustard
1/3	cup sour cream
1/4	cup raspberry-flavored vinegar
2	Tbls honey
1	cup cut frozen green beans, steamed
1	cup cooked sliced beets
1/2	cup sliced mushrooms
1/2	cup shredded carrots
8	oz cooked turkey breast, cut into julienne strips
4	cups mixed salad greens

Directions:
Mix mustard, sour cream, vinegar and honey in small bowl; refrigerate dressing until serving time. Arrange vegetables and turkey on large serving platter lined with salad greens. Drizzle with prepared dressing. Yield: 6 servings.

At The Market

1	onion
1	bulb garlic
1	lb ground turkey
1	box corn bread mix
1	(8-oz) container sour cream
1	(8-oz) can beets
1	(8-oz) carton mushrooms
1	(10-oz) bag shredded carrots
8	oz cooked turkey breast
1	bag prewashed, mixed salad greens
6	oranges

Per Serving: 213 calories, 21 g carbohydrate, 18 g protein, 8 g fat, 31 mg cholesterol, 402 mg sodium

Exchanges: 1 1/2 lean meats, 2 vegetables, 1 fat, 1 fruit

Kitchen Staples:
• vegetable oil • chicken broth • canned, stewed tomatoes • Dijon mustard •
• chili powder • ground red pepper • canned cannellini beans • canned corn •
• raspberry-flavored vinegar • honey • frozen green beans •

Greek Vegetable Salad

Salads

Asian Beef Salad

Sesame Breadsticks
Coconut Mandarin Parfait

Quick Meal Countdown:

1. Prepare parfait and chill.
2. Broil beef, let sit, then slice.
3. Prepare salad dressing.
4. Assemble Asian Beef Salad.

Asian Beef Salad

Prep Time: 5 minutes
Cook Time: 25 minutes

Ingredients:

Salad:

1 lb boneless beef top sirloin steak, cut 1-in thick

1/2 medium red onion, cut into thin wedges
3 Tbls chopped fresh cilantro
4 cups torn mixed salad greens, or thinly sliced napa cabbage
2 Tbls coarsely chopped peanuts (optional)

Citrus-Soy Dressing:

2 Tbls fresh lime juice
2 Tbls soy sauce
2 Tbls sugar
2 tsps dark sesame oil
1 green serrano chili pepper, seeded, finely chopped
1 large clove garlic, crushed

Directions:

Place steak on rack in broiler pan so surface of meat is 3 to 4 inches from heat. Broil 16 to 21 minutes for medium-rare to medium doneness, turning once. Let stand 10 minutes. Trim fat from steak and carve crosswise into slices. In a medium bowl, combine steak, onion and cilantro. In a small bowl, whisk together dressing ingredients. Pour over steak mixture; toss to coat. Arrange salad greens or cabbage on serving platter; top with steak mixture. Sprinkle with peanuts, if desired. Serve immediately.
Yield: 4 servings.

Per Serving: 226 calories, 9 g carbohydrate, 28 g protein, 9 g fat, 76 mg cholesterol, 597 mg sodium

Exchanges: 3 lean meats, 1 vegetable

Coconut Mandarin Parfait

Prep Time: 10 minutes
Chill Time: 20 minutes

Ingredients:

1	(3.4-oz) box instant coconut pudding
2	cups nonfat milk
2	cups canned mandarin oranges
4	gingersnap cookies, coarsely crushed
4	Tbls nonfat, nondairy whipped topping, thawed
2	gingersnap cookies, broken in half

Directions:

Prepare pudding mix with milk according to package directions. In each one of 4 goblets or parfait glasses, layer 1/4 cup pudding, 1 teaspoon crushed gingersnap and 1/4 cup mandarin oranges. Repeat. Garnish with 1 tablespoon whipped topping and 1/2 ginger-snap. Yield: 4 servings.

Per Serving:	215 calories, 46 g carbohydrate, 5 g protein, 2 g fat, 2 mg cholesterol, 426 mg sodium
Exchanges:	2 starches, 1/2 milk, 1 fruit

At The Market

1	lb boneless beef top sirloin
1	red onion
1	bunch fresh cilantro
1	bag prewashed, mixed salad greens or 1 head napa cabbage
1	(10-oz) bag peanuts (optional)
1	lime
1	green serrano chili pepper
1	bulb garlic
1	(4-oz) bag sesame breadsticks
1	pint nonfat milk

Kitchen Staples:

• soy sauce • sugar • dark sesame oil • coconut pudding mix •
• canned mandarin oranges • gingersnap cookies •
• nonfat, nondairy whipped topping •

Greek Vegetable Salad

Pita Wedges with Reduced Fat Hummus
Honey Nut Sundae

Quick Meal Countdown:
1. Prepare salad and dressing. Toss.
2. Just before serving, assemble sundaes.

Greek Vegetable Salad
Prep Time: 10 minutes

Ingredients:
1/2	head romaine lettuce, torn into bite-sized pieces
2	cups chopped tomatoes
1	small cucumber, thinly sliced
1	small onion, thinly sliced
1	small green bell pepper, seeded, cut into 1/4-in strips
4	oz reduced fat feta cheese, crumbled
2	tsps extra-virgin olive oil
1/4	cup red wine vinegar
1	Tbl water
1	large garlic clove, finely minced or pressed
1/2	tsp dried oregano, crushed
1/8	tsp freshly ground black pepper

Directions:
In a large bowl, toss together lettuce, tomatoes, cucumber, onion and green pepper. Top with cheese. In a separate small bowl, whisk together oil, vinegar, water, garlic, oregano and black pepper. Pour over salad and gently toss. Yield: 4 servings.

Per Serving:	141 calories, 15 g carbohydrate, 7 g protein, 7 g fat, 25 mg cholesterol, 331 mg sodium
Exchanges:	1 lean meat, 3 vegetables

Honey Nut Sundae

Prep Time: 5 minutes

Ingredients:
- 1   pint light vanilla ice cream
- 2   Tbls honey
- 2   Tbls chopped walnuts
-     Ground cinnamon

Directions:
Divide ice cream between 4 dessert dishes. Top each with 1/4 honey and nuts. Sprinkle with cinnamon. Yield: 4 servings.

Per Serving: 134 calories, 22 g carbohydrate, 3 g protein, 5 g fat, 8 mg cholesterol, 49 mg sodium

Exchanges: 1 1/2 starches, 1 fat

At The Market

- 1   *head romaine lettuce*
- 4   *tomatoes*
- 1   *cucumber*
- 1   *onion*
- 1   *green bell pepper*
- 1   *(4-oz) container reduced fat feta cheese*
- 1   *bulb garlic*
- 1   *(14-oz) package pita bread*
- 1   *(8-oz) container reduced fat hummus*

Kitchen Staples:
• extra-virgin olive oil • red wine vinegar • dried oregano • black pepper •
• light vanilla ice cream • honey • walnuts • ground cinnamon •

Hot Pork and Pear Salad
French Bread
Blueberry-Sauced Loaf Cake

Quick Meal Countdown:
1. Prepare pork and pear mixture.
2. Spoon pork mixture over salad greens.
3. Prepare blueberry sauce and serve over loaf cake.

Hot Pork and Pear Salad
Prep Time: 10 minutes
Cook Time: 10 minutes

Ingredients:
1	lb boneless pork chops, cut into 3 x 1/4-in strips
2	ripe, yet firm, pears
1	Tbl margarine
	Nonstick vegetable spray
1/4	cup cider vinegar
2	Tbls granulated sugar
1/2	tsp salt
1/4	cup raisins
6	cups mixed salad greens
1/4	cup walnuts, toasted and coarsely chopped

Directions:
Cut pork into 3 x 1/4-inch strips; set aside. Pare and core pears; cut into 12 slices. Melt margarine in a large, nonstick skillet; gently sauté pears until they are tender but still hold their shape. Remove from pan and set aside. Add nonstick vegetable spray to pan and stir-fry pork until lightly browned, about 3 minutes. Remove pork from pan; add vinegar, sugar and salt to pan juices; cook and stir until sugar dissolves. Return pork and pears to pan with raisins, stir gently to heat through. Put salad greens in a large salad bowl; spoon over pork mixture, toss. Garnish with walnuts. Yield: 6 servings.

Per Serving:	300 calories, 20 g carbohydrate, 20 g protein, 12 g fat, 50 mg cholesterol, 240 mg sodium
Exchanges:	2 lean meats, 1 vegetable, 1 fruit, 1 fat

Blueberry-Sauced Loaf Cake

Prep Time: 3 minutes

Ingredients:

1	(16-oz) light loaf cake
1	Tbl sugar-free apricot preserves
1	cup vanilla nonfat yogurt
1/2	cup (8 Tbls) fresh blueberries

Directions:

Cut cake in half. (Freeze remaining half for another use.) Cut cake into 4 equal pieces and place onto 4 dessert plates. In a small bowl, stir apricot preserves into yogurt. Spoon 1/4 cup mixture over each slice of cake. Top with 2 tablespoons blueberries. Yield: 4 servings.

Per Serving:	176 calories, 36 g carbohydrate, 6 g protein, 0 g fat, 1 mg cholesterol, 267 mg sodium
Exchanges:	2 starches

At The Market

1	lb boneless pork chops
2	pears
2	packages prewashed, mixed salad greens
1	loaf French bread
1	(16-oz) light loaf cake
1	carton blueberries

Kitchen Staples:

• margarine • nonstick vegetable spray • cider vinegar • granulated sugar •
• salt • raisins • walnuts • sugar-free apricot preserves • nonfat vanilla yogurt •

Summer Salad Mexicana
Baked Tortilla Chips with Salsa
Caribbean Cooler

Quick Meal Countdown:
1. Prepare tomatoes and filling, chill.
2. Assemble tomatoes and chill.
3. Prepare coolers.
4. Serve with chips and salsa.

Summer Salad Mexicana
Prep Time: 10 minutes
Cook Time: 10 minutes

Ingredients:
6	large tomatoes
3	(15-oz) cans black beans
1/2	cup canned corn, drained
1/2	cup chopped celery
1/2	cup chopped green bell pepper
1	green onion, including top, chopped
3	Tbls balsamic vinegar
1	Tbl finely chopped fresh cilantro leaves
1/8	tsp chili powder
1/8	tsp freshly ground black pepper
	Shredded lettuce
	Cilantro leaves for garnish

Directions:
Cut each tomato in half and scoop out centers. Discard tomato pulp and set aside tomato shells. Mix beans, corn, celery, green pepper and green onion in a medium-sized bowl. Gently stir in vinegar, cilantro, chili powder and pepper. Cover filling and tomato shells separately and chill. When ready to serve, place 2 tomato halves on each of 6 plates lined with a bed of shredded lettuce. Spoon an equal amount of bean mixture into each tomato half. Garnish with cilantro leaves. Yield: 6 servings.

Per Serving:	167 calories, 32 g carbohydrate, 9 g protein, 1 g fat, 0 mg cholesterol, 53 mg sodium
Exchanges:	1 very lean meat, 1 1/2 starches, 1 vegetable

Caribbean Cooler

Prep Time: 10 minutes
Cook Time: 2 minutes

Ingredients:
2   envelopes Knox® Unflavored Gelatine
2 1/2 cups orange juice, divided
2   cups sliced mango
2   medium ripe bananas
12   large ice cubes
     Mint spring, for garnish

Directions:
Sprinkle gelatine over 1/2 cup orange juice in small saucepan; let stand 1 minute. Stir gelatine over low heat until completely dissolved, about 1 minute. Blend mango slices, banana, remaining orange juice, gelatine mixture and ice cubes in electric blender at high speed until smooth. Pour into serving glasses; serve immediately. Yield: 6 servings.

At The Market

6	tomatoes
1	bunch celery
1	green bell pepper
1	bunch green onions
1	bunch fresh cilantro
1	bag shredded lettuce
1	(13 1/2-oz) bag baked tortilla chips
1	quart orange juice
1	mango
2	bananas
1	bunch fresh mint

Per Serving: 150 calories, 35 g carbohydrate, 4 g protein, 1 g fat, 0 mg cholesterol, 8 mg sodium

Exchanges: 1/2 very lean meat, 2 fruits

Kitchen Staples:
• canned black beans • canned corn • balsamic vinegar • chili powder •
• black pepper • salsa • unflavored gelatin •

Metric Conversion Tables

Metric Measure/Conversion

Approximate Conversion To Metric Measures

When You Know...	Multiply By...	To Find...	
	Mass (weight)		
ounces	28	grams	g
pounds	0.45	kilograms	kg
	(Volume)		
teaspoons	5	milliliters	ml
tablespoons	15	milliliters	ml
fluid ounces	30	milliliters	ml
cups	0.24	liters	l
pints	0.47	liters	l
quarts	0.95	liters	l
gallons	3.8	liters	l

1 calorie = 4.2 kilojoules

Cooking Measure Equivalents

Standard Cup	Volume (Liquid)	Liquid Solids (Butter)	Fine Powder (Flour)	Granular (Sugar)	Grain (Rice)
1	250 ml	200 g	140 g	190 g	150 g
3/4	188 ml	150 g	105 g	143 g	113 g
2/3	167 ml	133 g	93 g	127 g	100 g
1/2	125 ml	100 g	70 g	95 g	75 g
1/3	83 ml	67 g	47 g	63 g	50 g
1/4	63 ml	50 g	35 g	48 g	38 g
1/8	31 ml	25 g	18 g	24 g	19 g

Equivalent Measurements

3 teaspoons ....1 tablespoon

4 tablespoons ....1/4 cup

5 1/3 tablespoons ....1/3 cup

8 tablespoons ....1/2 cup

16 tablespoons...................................1 cup

2 tablespoons (liquid) ....1 ounce

1 cup....................................8 fluid ounces

2 cups ....1 pint
(16 fluid ounces)

4 cups...............................1 quart

4 quarts ....1 gallon

1/8 cup ....2 tablespoons

1/3 cup ....5 tablespoons
plus 1 teaspoon

2/3 cup ....10 tablespoons
plus 2 teaspoons

3/4 cup ....12 tablespoons

International Ingredient Substitutes

If the following ingredients aren't available in your country, try these ingredient substitutes:

Ingredient	Substitute Or Use
Almonds, teriyaki-flavored	Almonds (2 Tbls) with 1/8 tsp soy sauce
Beef, round tip	Beef eye-filet steak
Brown and wild rice mix	White and wild rice mix
Canned black beans	Cooked, black-eyed beans
Cappuccino-flavored, fat-free yogurt	Low fat vanilla yoghurt with 1 tsp coffee
Cilantro	Fresh coriander
Corn bread mix	Substitute other bread (1 starch, 1 fat exchange)
Frozen melon medley	Fresh melon medley
Green serrano chili pepper	Jalapeño chili pepper
Halibut	Turbot
Honey graham crackers	Substitute other fat-free cookie
Lemon bar mix	Low fat lemon muffin mix
Light fruit spread	Low-sugar jam
Light loaf cake	Sponge cake
Napa cabbage	Chinese cabbage
Oyster crackers	Saltine crackers
Papaya	Paw paw
Peppers, green/red	Capsicum, green/red
Romaine lettuce	Any green lettuce
Wheat pilaf (bulgar)	Burghal (hulled wheat)

Recipe Index

Acknowledgements

Jenny Craig would like to thank the companies and organizations listed below for the use of their recipes and photographs in this publication.

American Dry Bean Board

Bertolli

California Fresh Apricot Council

Gingerich Farms Products, Inc.

The Jel Sert Company

Kansas Beef Council

Kraft Foods, Inc.

McCormick & Company, Inc.

National Fisheries Institute

National Pork Producers Council

National Turkey Federation

The Oregon Raspberry and Blackberry Commission

Texas Beef Council

Tyson Foods, Inc.